MW01165271

Hope and a Future

The Coming Reformation in America

By Craig M. Kibler

PLC
PUBLICATIONS

Hope and a Future: The Coming Reformation in America

© 2006 by PLC Publications

PLC Publications
P.O. Box 2210
136 Tremont Park Drive
Lenoir, North Carolina 28645

PLC Publications books, monographs and other resources are available at special discounts in bulk purchases for educational and ministry use. For more details, contact:

Director of Publications
PLC Publications
P.O. Box 2210
136 Tremont Park Drive
Lenoir, North Carolina 28645

Call us at 1-800-368-0110

Or visit PLC Publications on the Web at www.resourcecatalog.org

Cover Illustration: Peter Frank, Pittsburgh, Pennsylvania
Cover Design: Joel McClure; HeuleGordon, Inc.; Grand Rapids, Michigan

Printed in the United States of America

Table of Contents

Foreword

The coming Reformation in America in these early years of the 21st century is being led not by the leaders of many of the Protestant mainline denominations but, rather, by independent groups and their allies around the world who are calling for the affirmation of traditional, orthodox Christianity in a pluralistic society heavily influenced by secular culture.

Within their own denominations, those calling for such an affirmation have become exiles, strangers and aliens. Speaking for many such people in the Protestant mainline, Episcopal Bishop Robert W. Duncan Jr. says, "We have been taken captive, against our will, to a place we did not wish to go."

This is a startling indictment of those denominational leaders who profess one thing in their ordination vows and then, in practice, demonstrate something entirely different. Over the years, for example, some of them have:

- Suggested that "creeds" should be chosen by the "democratic process" through accumulated human wisdom rather than through Biblically derived affirmations of faith.

- Denied Jesus Christ's eternal deity.

- Denied His atonement for the sins of the world.

- Denied Jesus' unique role as Savior.

- Rejected a "theistic" God.

- Denied the bodily resurrection and virgin birth of Christ.

- Espoused a moral code derived from modern human experience rather than the Bible.[1]

---

1. G.K. Chesterton; *Heretics: The Annotated Edition*; Edited by Craig M. Kibler (Reformation Press; Lenoir, N.C.; 2005); pp. 25-27.

At a time in history when a bold affirmation of a Biblical worldview to address the problems facing today's society is sorely needed, Church leaders have the power – and what always goes with power, the responsibility – to raise that standard. As people in the pews look to them to advise and lead them and guide the Church in these uncertain times, these Church leaders are called to be the captains of the gate barring Scriptural vacuity and its comrade in arms, moral ambiguity, from entering the policies of the their respective denominations.

Alas, many of those church leaders have abrogated that role and, instead, have infused their constituencies with timidity – getting majorities to meekly acquiesce to staff-generated and leadership-endorsed policies that perpetuate the bureaucratic institution's continuing slide into irrelevancy.

This theological drift has not abated with time. Indeed, many denominational leaders more and more have exacerbated it by embracing an increasingly cultural accommodation. The result has been a diminished proclamation of the Gospel of Jesus Christ and the rise of an institutionalized ideology that espouses cultural policies of the moment, such as unrestricted abortion and sexuality without limits.

That is why those independent groups and their allies are standing on the Word from which comes the strength to engage and change a culture drowning in a theology of cultural accommodation, the celebration of personal experience and the reasoning of the self. In so doing, these traditional, orthodox Christians are voicing a message of hope that the light of Christ still is shining in the darkness of the mainline communions.

"Many of us have found that committed Christian believers have more in common with believers in other mainline denominations than with some wayward forms of her own church leadership," Dr. Thomas C. Oden, a retired professor of Theology and Ethics at the Theological School and the Graduate School at Drew University, said during the historic 2002 Confessing The Faith Conference – the first-ever gathering of renewing and confessing Christians in North America.

"We seek to embody the unity of believing Christians in

mainline denominations, and to reaffirm classic orthodox Christianity. We are here to create our oneness in Jesus Christ, to learn from each other about how the Spirit is working among us in our various vineyards, and to ask the Spirit to guide us in discernment," he said, adding:

"To prevent further hemorrhaging of our churches, believers with all the mainline churches have formed confessing and renewing movements composed of people and congregations who exalt the Lordship of Jesus Christ and who adhere to classical Christian teaching of the Biblical faith, and who pray for the Spirit to strengthen the holy life. We call upon our church leaders, trustees of institutions, board members of boards and agencies, and the seminaries of our churches, to transmit the historic Christian faith."

That and other messages of the coming Reformation in America are expressed in the pages of this volume, which examines one of the many examples of renewal going on in this country. "Jesus Christ is our hope," Duncan told more than 2,500 participants at the first-ever international "Hope and a Future" conference on a cold, blustery November weekend in Pittsburgh.

"He is the whole of it," Duncan said. "He is the sum and substance of it. One of the two 'conference hymns' is *In Christ Alone My Hope is Found*. If we keep Jesus before our eyes, we will be able to face any challenge that comes our way."

Although sponsored by the Anglican Communion Network, the issues discussed during the conference are universal to many of the Protestant mainline denominations. The Network was created in 2003 by Duncan and other conservative bishops after the denomination elevated a homosexual man, V. Gene Robinson, to bishop of New Hampshire and gave tacit approval to same-sex blessings.

"Global Christianity is also reforming and re-forming," Duncan said, echoing the themes expressed by other confessing and renewal groups. "Those who have been divided from one another are being brought together, both within orthodox Anglicanism and within the wider Christian family. Mission is being reshaped and reinvigorated everywhere and the center of world

Christianity is shifting south.

"To be here is to choose to soldier on. ... For everyone in this hall, we are continuing to deal with choosing Jesus first: Jesus above culture, Jesus above comfort, Jesus above property, Jesus above family and friends, Jesus above any other security, Jesus above a wayward North American Church. We are here to confirm our choice for truth above accommodation."

That is the method of these independent groups and their allies around the world. They are speaking the one truth of Jesus Christ plainly and with the authority of Scripture to a society that, in many ways, has lost its bearings and is searching for the solace that only is possible in the Word, incarnate and written. "Faith," John Calvin says, "is never without a fight. ... My fiercest battles must be against my own inclinations."

This message, this food for the soul, is strikingly relevant today – an age of relativism, societal decay and shifting standards. As polarizing differences over Christology, Biblical authority, sexual ethics and other theological issues continue to threaten the peace, unity and purity of many of the Protestant mainline denominations, these groups are standing up and proclaiming: "Who do you say that I am?"[2] and "Choose you this day."[3]

They are asserting, boldly and without equivocation, that Jesus Christ alone is the way, the truth and the life for the entire world. Period. They proclaim that "I am" is eternal and unchanging, and that the only real freedom of conscience for Christians is to either choose or not choose to build their lives on this singular truth. Anything less opens the door, in both interpretation and practice, to "I am, maybe."

The prospect of something less, and the resultant anxieties and perplexities, is being answered by these groups as they seek to stem their respective bureaucratic institutions accelerating slide down the slippery slope to irrelevancy by doggedly persisting in bearing faithful witness in the face of overwhelming rejection and ridicule.

---

2.   Matthew 16:13-15.

3.   Joshua 24:15.

And what about those people whose decisions *de jure* validated those staff-generated and leadership-endorsed policies that continue sliding much of the Protestant mainline down that slippery slope? After all, they are honorable men and women, well-meaning and well-intentioned, acting out of an expressed love for their respective institutions.

The only pertinent response comes from Shakespeare's *Julius Caesar.* Paraphrasing the speech by Brutus in which he explains why he believed Caesar had to die, "It's not that they loved Jesus Christ less, but that they loved the institution more."

In the final analysis, nothing can save the mainline denominations if they will not save themselves. If they lose faith in Jesus Christ alone, in Scripture's capacity to guide and govern our lives; if they lose their will to proclaim the Gospel to all corners of the world, then their slide into irrelevancy will be complete.

If appeasers from within and without daily exert a more aggressive and activist cultural accommodation, and the people in the pews remain paralyzed by a misplaced sense of unity or remain dazed by exhaustion brought on by battle fatigue defending the Permanent Things, then complete irrelevancy will be swift and final.

Thankfully, in answer to constant prayer that may yet convert those responsible for the state of the Protestant mainline today, that day is not here – as the work of these independent groups and their allies are demonstrating. If traditional, orthodox Christians all across this country, in congregations large and small, stand up and proclaim, "We support the new Reformation," then the Protestant mainline denominations' return to being the Church God has called them to be is not far off.

That road will be hard, and those faithful witnesses traveling it will be beset on all sides, but the source of their strength, the bright light they are following and the ultimate outcome is clear:

My grace is sufficient for you, for my power is made perfect in weakness.[4]

---

4. 2 Corinthians 12:9.

I know the plans I have
for you, says the Lord, plans
for welfare and not for evil,
to give you hope and a future.

Jeremiah 29:11

CHAPTER ONE

'The logjam is about to break'

"The logjam is about to break," Episcopal Bishop Robert W. Duncan Jr. said at the opening of the first-ever international conference "Hope and a Future." "The way forward for Biblical and missionary Anglicans – and Christians – is increasingly clear and involves all of us together."

"This conference," Duncan said in his keynote address, "comes at a *kairos* moment in Anglican development, in Western civilization and in Christian history. We have gathered here to be encouraged, to be challenged and to be sent."

Early in the planning for the conference, Duncan said, "God gave that early committee the Scripture verse and the reference out of which the conference title and the conference message spring:

> I know the plans I have for you, says the Lord, plans for welfare and not for evil, to give you hope and a future.[1]

"It is to this verse that I want to turn as I give one part of the overview for this conference," he said.

"Our identity as orthodox Anglican Christians in North America is as exiles, strangers and aliens. The beautiful city of

---

1. Jeremiah 29:11.

classical Anglicanism, in which we were raised or to which we had found our way, now lies in ruins. We have been taken captive, against our will, to a place we did not wish to go. On our best days, and at our most positive, we might describe ourselves as pilgrims, on a journey from the place we had known to the one we trust God will give us, but we are very far – very far – from having arrived. This is a very difficult time for us all, even if we have been among the few who have been able to hold on to much of what we had.

"No matter what the particulars of the local circumstances from which we have come, every one of us is clear that we are very far from the realization of that united, Biblical and missionary Anglicanism that is our vision, at least in penultimate terms. Ultimately, there is not one of us here who yearns for anything less than the heavenly city, but penultimately our sights are set on a united, Biblical and missionary Anglicanism, and we are not ashamed to admit it or to admit how far we still have to go. But this conference is a step, corporately for us all and individually for each one who has sacrificed to come and who is prepared to claim our hope and decide for our future."

Duncan offered the participants "three encouragements, three warnings and three choices" to consider as the conference proceeded. The three encouragements were that Jesus Christ is our hope; that Anglicanism is reforming and re-forming; and that the future is the mission.

"Jesus Christ is our hope," he said. "He is the whole of it. He is the sum and substance of it. One of the two 'conference hymns' is *In Christ Alone My Hope is Found*. If we keep Jesus before our eyes, we will be able to face any challenge that comes our way.

"Global Christianity is also reforming and re-forming," Duncan said. "Those who have been divided from one another are being brought together, both within orthodox Anglicanism and within the wider Christian family. Mission is being reshaped and reinvigorated everywhere and the center of world Christianity is shifting south.

"When asked about what we could do in the midst of our

present sufferings, our dear brother Archbishop Henry Orombi said, 'You can do the mission.' Jesus' instructions to feed the hungry, give drink to the thirsty, welcome the stranger, visit the sick, go to those in prison, clothe the naked – as well as to proclaim his salvation to all creation – apply to all seasons, good and bad. If we want Jesus' future to come, the third encouragement is that to focus on the mission – every last one of us – is the quickest, happiest and most fulfilling way to get there."

Duncan said Jeremiah and the wider Biblical witness about exiles and pilgrims provide three warnings. The first is about impatience.

"When are we going to get there?" he asked. "The English word 'patience' is built on the Latin verb meaning 'to suffer.' We in the West are not willing to suffer. Ours is a very sick culture addicted to painkillers. We want to be there now. If God doesn't deliver us from our fears, anxieties, discouragements and losses now, then our lips are filled with murmuring. How are we different from the children of Israel in their long-ago wilderness? There is not one of us who does not murmur. The Biblical witness that is that murmuring – and the impatience out of which it grows – only lengthens the purgatory of the wilderness."

Duncan's second warning was about idolatry.

"When the impatience becomes unbearable, when despair overtakes us, when we reach the point where we just cannot see how our God can be trusted any more for the outcome," he said, "we turn to false gods. We melt down what we have and make a golden calf. The calf can be accommodation, the calf can be autonomy, the calf can be sullen inaction. What calf have you set up? What calf have I set up? Jeremiah warns the exiles that the time of exile will not pass quickly, and that those who say it will are false prophets. Settle yourselves. Trust God for his plan and his deliverance in his time."

Duncan's third warning was about self-righteousness.

"It is not just someone else's sin that got us here," he said. "It is our sin, our complicity, our unfaithfulness. It is not about pharaoh any more. He has been severely punished, and will know eternal separation. But we are God's special people and it is our sin that we must deal with, and that he is dealing with. The call for repentance is a call to us. We have a log in our own eye. We will not get out of this wilderness by blaming others or setting up false gods but, only by genuine repentance and by a return to our first love, will we be ready to enter the Promised Land or be restored to the geography of the land we once knew."

He then spoke about people making a choice. "To be here is to make a choice," Duncan said. "To be here is to choose to soldier on. There are three choices this conference, and our present exile, implores. The first choice is for truth over accommodation. For everyone in this hall, we are continuing to deal with choosing Jesus first: Jesus above culture, Jesus above comfort, Jesus above property, Jesus above family and friends, Jesus above any other security, Jesus above a wayward North American Church. We are here to confirm our choice for truth above accommodation. This is the evangelical choice."

He said the second choice is for accountability over autonomy. "Freedom, like truth, is a passion that all of us share," Duncan said. "But the vast danger here is that we will get stuck in our freedom. Forty years of Anglican splits and splinters tells the story only too well. Autonomy is every bit as much a danger as accommodation. We are here to make a choice for accountability over autonomy. This is the catholic choice."

The third choice, he said, is for "the mission over sullen inaction. Is your congregation a church-planting congregation? Is your congregation partnered with a Global South diocese? Is your congregation functioning in local needs-based evangelism? Are you personally engaged in a Matthew 25 ministry? Have you personally led anyone else to a saving faith in Jesus Christ? Have you challenged those around you to choose this day?[2] Are you trapped in 'Ain't it awful?' or 'What can we possibly do?' or the escape of self-absorption? We are Holy Spirit people: people who have been gifted, 'charismed.' We are here to elect the mission over sullen inaction. This is the charismatic choice."

"We are here," Duncan said, "to model a united, Biblical and

---

2.   Joshua 24:15.

missionary way of being Anglicans; to repent for our impatience, idolatry and self-righteousness; to choose truth and accountability and mission; to begin to set a wholesome and reformed DNA in place for a movement that is evangelical and catholic and charismatic, and recognizably Anglican and passionately Christian; to allow ourselves to admit that a new day is dawning."

CHAPTER TWO

'Historic alliance proclaimed'

Organizers of the first-ever international conference "Hope and a Future" called it a showcase for an "historic alliance between the American evangelical mainstream and Anglicanism in the Global South."

Episcopal Bishop Robert W. Duncan Jr. said the conference was to focus on the renewal of North American Anglicanism and "the rebirth of a Biblical, missionary and united Anglicanism."

The Rev. Dr. Leslie P. Fairfield, a professor of church history at Trinity Episcopal School for Ministry in Ambridge, Penn., said, "I believe that our identity and mission as orthodox American Anglicans lies in this historic alliance."

"Our institutional arrangements with the Episcopal Church will take whatever shape they may," Fairfield said. "The process will be painful. But let's not get bogged down in that mess. It's a choice between morass or mission. We need to make the mental shift now, and lean into our future. And our future lies in this mission-partnership with the American evangelical mainstream and the Anglican Churches of the Global South."

Duncan, in a letter to participants, wrote:

"To exiles 2,600 years ago, our God spoke about his good plans, about his desire for their welfare, and about 'Hope and a Future' (Jeremiah 29:11). There has been much heartache, persecution, anxiety and loss among us faithful North American Anglicans in recent years. But I believe the dust is settling and that we can begin to see the outlines of what, by God's grace, is emerging."

The reason for the conference, Duncan said, was "because we need Jesus and one another more than ever. In times of storm and struggle, it is our support for one another, with God's grace, that gets us through."

"Because the whole world is watching," he said. "From Singapore to Kampala to Rome to Los Angeles, there is the sense that the attendance and the events at this conference will be an indicator of the viability of a reformed and realigned North American Anglicanism. Because the logjam is about to break.

"The way forward for Biblical and missionary Anglicans – and Christians – is increasingly clear and involves all of us together," Duncan said. "Because you have been called. No matter where you are or how insignificant you believe the contribution you have to make, come claim your part and come understand what is your hope and your future."

CHAPTER THREE

Worst-case scenario strategies dismissed

The Anglican Communion Network is dismissing as "conspiracy theories" reports that, should the Episcopal Church (USA) splinter after its next General Convention, a group is making plans that include the attempted removal from office of bishops and lay leaders affiliated with the network.

Network officials, at the time of the "Hope and a Future" conference, claimed that it is comprised of 10 dioceses and six convocations stretching from coast to coast, border to border, in the United States representing 200,000 members in more than 800 congregations. They said the Network has received support throughout the Anglican Communion, including encouragement from the Archbishop of Canterbury, while 14 other leaders – representing 75 percent of the world's 60 million Anglicans – have offered their recognition and pledged the full weight of their ministries to the Network.

The Living Church magazine, meanwhile, reported that a group called Via Media USA was working on a "worst-case scenario" for the next Episcopal Church (USA) General Convention, and that its plans call for replacing bishops and lay leaders with people the organization believes will remain obedient to the Constitution and canons of the General Convention.

Commenting on this "day-after" strategy, Joan R. Gunderson,

who is listed at the end of the four-page document as temporary secretary for the group's steering committee, told *The Living Church* magazine that, "The steering committee meeting was not open to the public and the minutes were not intended for public release."

Gunderson, who also is vice president of Progressive Episcopalians of Pittsburgh, said the "strategy discussion" was part of a "what if" contingency plan based on a "worst-case scenario" in which, after the 75th General Convention, the Episcopal Church would remain in a smaller Anglican Communion with the majority of Anglican provinces in Africa breaking communion with the See of Canterbury and the network bishops seeking to follow.

"What will be our response the 'Day After' when the bishops start announcing they are in a 'new' Anglican Communion and the Network is 'recognized' as the only legitimate expression of the A.C. in North America?" the steering committee asked, according to the draft minutes of its meeting.

"'Blank presentments' for abandonment of communion should be prepared in advance along with documentation to have the 'see' declared vacant and an 'interim bishop' appointed," the draft minutes reported.

The interim bishop then would be given a previously prepared request for a special convention "so that vacant spots in diocesan government can be filled (trustees, council, standing committee, commission on ministry, etc.)," according to the draft minutes.

The Network, in a statement, said it "thanks *The Living Church* magazine for reporting on what Via Media USA's acting secretary calls its worst-case scenario. Talk of blank presentment forms, and consulting with the presiding bishop about replacing duly elected bishops, does indeed qualify as anticipating and preparing for the worst. The Network has been the frequent subject of conspiracy theories, and we are content to let our actions speak for themselves."

"To the extent that the Episcopal Church insists on walking apart from the broader Anglican Communion, the Network intends to strengthen Anglican bonds of affection. As we look toward the General Convention, we recall this warning to the early church:

> "Come now, you who say, 'Today or tomorrow we will go to such and such a town and spend a year there, doing business and making money.' Yet you do not even know what tomorrow will bring. What is your life? For you are a mist that appears for a little while and then vanishes. Instead you ought to say, 'If the Lord wishes, we will live and do this or that.' As it is, you boast in your arrogance; all such boasting is evil. Anyone, then, who knows the right thing to do and fails to do it, commits sin."[1]

The reports also were strongly condemned by the American Anglican Council, a renewal group that affirms Biblical authority and Christian orthodoxy within the Anglican Communion.

The group, in a statement, said Via Media USA "is planning attacks against the Anglican Communion Network dioceses and bishops at the conclusion of General Convention. It is reported that they will have fill-in-the-blank deposition documents against ACN bishops, as well as true-church-lawsuit documents, ready to fill in for court litigation. If Via Media's plans become a reality, every orthodox bishop and diocese will be ousted, leaving dioceses with rogue bishops and diocesan commissions. The Biblically faithful within those dioceses would be held captive and lose their affiliation with the worldwide Anglican Communion."

"Via Media's exposed plot to supplant ACN bishops is outrageous and unconscionable," the statement said. "It is a travesty for a group bent upon abandoning any semblance of Anglican faith and order to call itself 'via media.' The 'via media' of Anglicanism historically refers to the Church of England's middle ground between Roman Catholicism and Free Church Protestantism, and emphasizes unity based on the essentials of faith as expressed in Scripture. To misappropriate this Anglican

---

1. James 4:14-17.

terminology and apply it to an entity established to promote a false gospel is beyond the pale.

"Since its inception, Via Media has served as a pawn of 815 [the Episcopal Church's national office], Integrity USA, Every Voice Network, and other radical revisionists intent upon transforming the Episcopal Church into a religion devoid of Christian faith, doctrine and practice," the statement said. "While espousing a mantra of tolerance and diversity, the organization has now been exposed as a body committed to dismantling dioceses that uphold Scriptural faith and historic Anglican doctrine. Via Media clearly has no desire to walk together with the Anglican Communion; nor does it respect the mind of the Communion on matters of sexuality. Rather, it has plotted and schemed with unparalleled duplicity to seize control of dioceses, thereby usurping legitimate episcopal and diocesan authority.

"If Frank Griswold, Episcopal Church (USA) Chancellor David Booth Beers and 815 are not complicit in this scandalous plan, they need to publicly repudiate Via Media's strategy and break all contact with Via Media groups," the statement said, adding:

"Tragically, there is little hope that the Episcopal Church (USA) will pull away from Via Media. Let us not forget that a group of Episcopal Church (USA) bishops has established a special task force to develop strategies for ensuring that no churches leaving the Episcopal Church as a matter of conscience retain their property. The formation of this task force has been made public; now, Via Media's intentions have been revealed. What other secret plans are being plotted behind closed doors that have not yet been leaked? We encourage those who have knowledge of such plans and proposals to come forward and place them in the public sector so that all can be forewarned."

CHAPTER FOUR

North American networks recognized

Two Anglican networks, which were formed in opposition to the Episcopal Church (USA)'s decision in 2003 to accept an openly gay bishop and give tacit approval to same-sex blessings, have been recognized by the Archbishop of Canterbury as "full members of the Anglican Communion."

The announcement by Bishop Robert W. Duncan Jr. was applauded at the opening of the "Hope and a Future" conference, which Duncan has said will focus on the renewal of North American Anglicanism and "the rebirth of a Biblical, missionary and united Anglicanism."

"Just 13 days ago, at Ain El-Suhknah (Egypt) on the Red Sea, I received a tap on the back, and turned around to be embraced by Archbishop of Canterbury Rowan Williams," Duncan told the crowd. "Within minutes of that embrace, Dr. Williams spoke these words to the delegates of South-South Encounter III: 'I recognize all the bishops, priests and people of the Networks [of the United States and Canada] as full members of the Anglican Communion.' It was a welcome and long-awaited verbal embrace and public recognition for us who gather here today."

A communique from the 103 delegates from the Global South – comprising Africa, South and South East Asia, the West

Indies and South America – who met in Ain El-Suhknah, also praised the archbishop's recognition.

"We are grateful that the Archbishop of Canterbury publicly recognized the Anglican Communion Network in the USA and the Anglican Network in Canada as faithful members of the Anglican Communion," the communique said.

Duncan was more specific in highlighting the unity made clear in Williams' statement.

"What is more significant still is that the plain sense of the archbishop's words means that someone who stands with us – even if outside the Episcopal Church (USA) or the Anglican Church of Canada – is an Anglican," he said. "That is not hope, or the future, that is the present! The old exclusive franchises are no more. A new day is dawning. The day has a very long way to run, but the day is begun. Praise God!

"The delegates of the entire South-to-South Encounter III," Duncan said, "spoke these words two days later: 'Global South is committed to provide our recognition, energy, prayers and experience to the Networks in the U.S.A. and Canada, the Convocation of Nigerian Anglicans in the U.S.A., those who make Common Cause and the Missionary District that is gathering congregations that circumstances have pressed out of the Episcopal Church (USA). We are heartened by the bold witness of their people. ...'

"We who are gathered here – all of us – are at one with the vast majority of Anglicans worldwide, and they are at one with us," Duncan said. "Our day is dawning, right here, right now. Ain-el-Suhknah, in Arabic, means 'the place of the crossing.' The reference is to the great Exodus of God's people from their land of bondage. We rejoice in that defining story, and in the emerging outlines of our own. But we also must soberly remember that it is a very long way to the Promised Land, and that manifold temptations will assault and assail us in the wilderness of this new day dawning. We must not turn to the right or to the left, but keep our eyes, our hearts, our feet, and our actions steady behind the pillar and the cloud that are the Lord's singular leading for this day."

The communiqué from the Third Anglican Global South-to-South Encounter also was critical of what it called "unchecked revisionist teaching and practices which undermine the divine authority of the Holy Scripture."

"The Anglican Communion is severely wounded by the witness of errant principles of faith and practice which in many parts of our Communion have adversely affected our efforts to take the Gospel to those in need of God's redeeming and saving love," the statement said.

"Un-Scriptural innovations of North American and some western provinces on issues of human sexuality undermine the basic message of redemption and the power of the Cross to transform lives. The leaders of these provinces disregard the plain teaching of Scripture and reject the traditional interpretation of tenets in the historical Creeds."

The leaders recommitted themselves to the authority of the Word of God and their endorsement of the concept and formulation of an Anglican Covenant "rooted in the Windsor Report."

"We are seeking a Covenant that is rooted in historic faith and formularies, and that provides a Biblical foundation for our life, ministry and mission as a Communion.... It is envisaged that once the Covenant is approved by the Communion, provinces that enter into the Covenant shall be mutually accountable, thereby providing an authentic fellowship within the Communion."

The statement concluded that the Episcopal Church (USA) and the Anglican Church of Canada had not taken the necessary steps to meet the requirements of the Windsor Report.

"Regrettably, even at the meeting of the Anglican Consultative Council in Nottingham (United Kingdom) in 2005, we see no evidence that both the Episcopal Church (USA) and the Anglican Church of Canada are willing to accept the generally accepted teaching, nor is there evidence that they are willing to turn back from their innovations."

The statement called for "urgent and serious" implementation of the recommendations of the Windsor Report in order to prevent a split in the Anglican Communion.

"Un-Scriptural and unilateral decisions, especially on moral issues, tear the fabric of our Communion and require appropriate discipline at every level to maintain our unity," the statement said, adding:

"While the Global South calls for the errant provinces to be disciplined, we will continue to pray for all who embrace these erroneous teachings that they will be led to repentance and restoration."

The full text of the statement, which addressed a wide range of issues, is as follows:

The Third Anglican Global South to South Encounter

The Third Anglican South-to-South Encounter has graphically demonstrated the coming of age of the Church of the Global South. We are poignantly aware that we must be faithful to God's vision of one, holy, catholic and apostolic Church. We do not glory in our strength, but in God's strength. We do not shrink from our responsibility as God's people because of our weaknesses, but we trust God to demonstrate his power through our weakness. We thank God for moving us forward to serve him in such a time as this.

A. Preamble

1. A total of 103 delegates of 20 provinces in the Global South (comprising Africa, South and South East Asia, the West Indies and South America), representing approximately two-thirds of the Anglican Communion, met for the 3rd Global South to South Encounter from 25-30 October 2005 at Ain El-Sukhna by the Red Sea in Egypt. The theme of the Encounter was "One, Holy, Catholic and Apostolic Church: Being a Faithful Church for Such a Time As This."

2. We deeply appreciated the Archbishop of Canterbury for the time he spent with us, his listening ear and encouraging words. We took to heart his insight that the four marks of the Church are not attributes we possess as our own right, nor goals to attain by human endeavor, but they are

expressed in us as we deeply focus on Jesus Christ, who is the Source of them all.[1]

3. We were really warmed by the welcome that we received here by the president, the government and the people of Egypt. We valued the great efforts made by the state security personnel who are making the land of Egypt a secure and safe place to all her visitors. We were touched by the warm hospitality of the Diocese of Egypt.

4. We have witnessed in Egypt a wonderful model for warm relations between Christians and Muslims. We admire the constructive dialogue that is happening between the two faiths. We appreciated the attendance of the Grand Imam of Al-Azhar, Dr Mohammed Said Tantawi, the representative of Pope Shenouda III and other religious leaders at the State Reception to launch our Encounter. We were encouraged by their wise contributions.

B. We Gathered

5. We gathered to seek the face of God, to hear his Word afresh and to be renewed by his Spirit for total obedience to Christ, who is Lord of the Church. That is why the gathering was called an "Encounter," rather than a conference. The vital question we addressed was: What does it mean to be one, holy, catholic and apostolic Church in the midst of all the challenges facing the world and the Church?

6. The world of the Global South is riddled with the pain of political conflict, tribal warfare and bloodshed. The moral and ethical foundations of several of our societies are being shaken. Many of our nations are beset by problems of poverty, ignorance and sickness, particularly the HIV and AIDS that threaten millions, especially in Africa. In addition to that, thousands of people have suffered from severe drought in Africa, earthquakes in South Asia, and hurricanes in the Americas – we offer our support and prayers to them.

---

1. John 17:17-21.

7. Apart from the world condition, our own Anglican Communion sadly continues to be weakened by unchecked revisionist teaching and practices which undermine the divine authority of the Holy Scripture. The Anglican Communion is severely wounded by the witness of errant principles of faith and practice which, in many parts of our Communion, have adversely affected our efforts to take the Gospel to those in need of God's redeeming and saving love.

8. Notwithstanding these difficult circumstances, several parts of our Communion in the Global South are witnessing the transforming power of the Gospel and the growth of the Church. The urgency of reaching vast multitudes in our nations for Christ is pressing at our door and the fields are ready for harvest.

9. Surrounded by these challenges and seeking to discover afresh our identity, we decided to dig deeper into God's Word and into the tradition of the Church to learn how to be faithful to God's gift and call to be his one, holy, catholic and apostolic people. We deliberately chose to meet in Egypt for two reasons:

    a. Biblically, Egypt features prominently in the formative period of the calling of God's people.[2] Moreover, Egypt was part of the cradle that bore the entry of the Savior into the world.[3]

    b. Meeting by the Red Sea, we could not help but be inspired by the historic crossing of God's people into the realm where he purposed to make them a "light to the nations."[4] Part of that blessing was fulfilled when Alexandria became a center of early Christianity, where church fathers formulated and held on to the Christian faith through the early centuries.

---

2. Exodus 19.
3. Hosea 11:1; Matthew 2:13-15.
4. Isaiah 42:6.

C. We Discovered Afresh

10. We discovered afresh the depth and richness of our roots in the one, holy, catholic and apostolic Church. Carefully researched papers were presented at the Encounter in the context of worship, prayer, Bible study and mutual sharing. We recognize the dynamic way in which the four marks of the Church are inextricably interwoven. The salient truths we encountered inspired us and provided a basis for knowing what God requires of us.

The Church is One

11. The Church is called to be one. Our unity is willed by our Lord Jesus Christ himself, who prayed that we "all might be one."[5] A great deal of confusion has arisen out of misunderstanding that prayer and the concept of unity. For centuries, the Church has found unity in the Person and teaching of Jesus Christ, as recorded in Scripture. We are one in him, and that binds us together. The foundation and expression of our unity is found in Jesus Christ as Savior and Lord.

12. While our unity may be expressed in institutional life, our unity is grounded in our living relationship with the Christ of Scripture. Unity is ever so much more than sharing institutionally. When we are "in Christ," we find that we are in fellowship with others who also are in him. The fruit of that unity is that we faithfully manifest the life and love of Christ to a hurting and groaning world.[6]

13. Christian unity is premised on truth and expressed in love. Both truth and love compel us to guard the Gospel and stand on the supreme authority of the whole Word of God. The boundary of family identity ends within the boundary of the authentic Word of God.

---

5. John 17:20-21.
6. Romans 8:18-22.

The Church is Holy

14. The Church of Jesus Christ is called to be holy. All Christians are to participate in the sanctification of their lives through submission, obedience and cooperation with the Holy Spirit. Through repentance, the Church can regain her rightful position of being holy before God. We believe concurrently that holiness is imparted to us through the life, ministry, death and resurrection of our Lord Jesus Christ.[7] He shares his holiness with us and invites us to be conformed to his likeness.

15. A holy Church is prepared to be a "martyr" Church. Witness unto death is how the Early Church articulated holiness in its fullest sense.[8]

The Church is Catholic

16. The Catholic faith is the universal faith that was "once for all" entrusted to the apostles and handed down subsequently from generation to generation.[9] Therefore, every proposed innovation must be measured against the plumb line of Scripture and the historic teaching of the Church.

17. Catholicity carries with it the notion of completeness and wholeness. Thus, in the church catholic, "when one part suffers, every part suffers with it."[10] The local church expresses its catholicity by its devotion to apostolic teaching, its attention to prayer and the sacrament, its warm and caring fellowship and its growth through evangelism and mission.[11]

The Church is apostolic

18. The Church is apostolic in its doctrine and teaching. The

7. Hebrews 10:21-23.
8. Acts 22:20; Revelation 2:13, 12:11.
9. Jude 3.
10. 1 Corinthians 12:26.
11. Acts 2:42-47.

apostolic interpretation of God's salvation plan effected in Christ Jesus is binding on the Church. God established the Church on the "foundation of the apostles and prophets with Christ Jesus himself as the chief cornerstone."[12]

19. The Church is apostolic in its mission and service. "As the Father has sent me, so I send you."[13] In each generation, he calls bishops in apostolic succession[14] to lead the Church out into mission, to teach the truth and to defend the faith. Accountability to God, to those God places over us and to the flock, is an integral part of church leadership.

D. We Commit

20. As a result of our Encounter, we emerge with a clearer vision of what the Church is called to be and to do, with a renewed strength to pursue that vision. Specifically, we made commitments in the following areas.

The Authority of the Word of God

21. Scripture demands, and Christian history has traditionally held, that the standard of life, belief, doctrine, and conduct is the Holy Scripture. To depart from apostolic teaching is to tamper with the foundation and to undermine the basis of our unity in Christ. We express full confidence in the supremacy and clarity of Scripture, and pledge full obedience to the whole counsel of God's Word.

22. We in the Global South endorse the concept of an Anglican Covenant (rooted in the Windsor Report) and commit ourselves as full partners in the process of its formulation. We are seeking a Covenant that is rooted in historic faith and formularies, and that provides a Biblical foundation for our life, ministry and mission as a Communion. It is envisaged

---

12. Ephesians 2:20.

13. John 20:21.

14. Ephesians 4:11-12.

that once the Covenant is approved by the Communion, provinces that enter into the Covenant shall be mutually accountable, thereby providing an authentic fellowship within the Communion.

23. Anglicans of the Global South have discovered a vibrant spiritual life based on Scripture and empowered by the Spirit that is transforming cultures and communities in many of our provinces. It is to this life that we seek to be formed and found fully faithful. We reject the expectation that our lives in Christ should conform to the misguided theological, cultural and sociological norms associated with sections of the West.

Mission and Ministry

24. Churches in the Global South commit to pursue networking with one another to add strength to our mission and ministry. We will continue to explore appropriate structures to facilitate and support this.

25. Shared theological foundations are crucial to authentic fellowship and partnership in mission and ministry. In that light, we welcome the initiative to form the Council of Anglican Provinces of the Americas and the Caribbean (CAPAC). It is envisaged that CAPAC will not only provide a foundation on the historic formularies of Anglican faith, but also provide a structure with which member churches can carry out formal ministry partnerships with confidence.

26. Global South is committed to provide our recognition, energy, prayers and experience to the Networks in the U.S.A. and Canada, the Convocation of Nigerian Anglicans in the U.S.A., those who make Common Cause and the Missionary District that is gathering congregations that circumstances have pressed out of the Episcopal Church (USA). We are heartened by the bold witness of their people. We are grateful that the Archbishop of Canterbury publicly recognized the Anglican Communion Network in the U.S.A. and the Anglican Network in Canada as faithful

members of the Anglican Communion.

27. As for the other provinces and dioceses around the world that remain steadfastly committed to this faith, we look forward to further opportunities to partner with them in the propagation of the Gospel. We also will support those orthodox dioceses and congregations which are under difficult circumstances because of their faithfulness to the Word. We appreciate the recent action of the Primate of the Southern Cone, who acted to stabilize the volatile situation in Recife, Brazil. In this regard, we take this opportunity to acknowledge the immense contribution of the Primate of South East Asia to the development of the Global South and to the preservation of orthodoxy across the worldwide Anglican Communion.

Theological Education

28. In order to provide teaching that preserves the faith and fits our context, it is crucial to update the curricula of our theological institutions in the Global South to reflect our theological perspective and mission priorities. We note from the All Africa Bishops Conference their concern that far too many Western theological education institutions have become compromised and are no longer suitable for training leaders for our provinces. We call for the realignment of our priorities in such a way as to hasten the full establishment of adequate theological education institutions across the Global South so that our leaders can be appropriately trained and equipped in our own context. We aim to develop our leaders in Biblical and theological training, and seek to nurture indigenous theologians. We will provide information on institutions in the Global South, and we will encourage these institutions to explore ways to provide bursaries and scholarships.

The Current Crisis provoked by North American Intransigence

29. The un-Scriptural innovations of North American and some

Western provinces on issues of human sexuality undermine the basic message of redemption and the power of the Cross to transform lives. These departures are a symptom of a deeper problem, which is the diminution of the authority of Holy Scripture. The leaders of these provinces disregard the plain teaching of Scripture and reject the traditional inter-pretation of tenets in the historical Creeds.

30. This Encounter endorses the perspectives on communion life found in sections A & B of the Windsor Report, and encourages all provinces to comply with the request from the Primates' Communiqué in February 2005, which states: *"We therefore request all provinces to consider whether they are willing to be committed to the inter-dependent life of the Anglican Communion understood in the terms set out in these sections of the report."*

31. The Windsor Report rightly points out that the path to restoring order requires that either the innovating provinces/dioceses conform to historic teaching, or the offending provinces will by their actions be choosing to walk apart. Paragraph 12 of the Primates Communiqué says: *"Whilst there remains a very real question about whether the North American churches are willing to accept the same teaching on matters of sexual morality as is gener-ally accepted elsewhere in the Communion, the underlying reality of our communion in God the Holy Trinity is obscured, and the effectiveness of our common mission severely hindered."*

32. Regrettably, even at the meeting of the Anglican Consulta-tive Council (ACC) in Nottingham in 2005, we see no evi-dence that both the Episcopal Church (USA) and the Angli-can Church of Canada are willing to accept the generally accepted teaching, nor is there evidence that they are will-ing to turn back from their innovations.

33. Further, the struggles of the Communion have only been exacerbated by the lack of concrete progress in the imple-mentation of the recommendations of the Windsor Report.

The slow and inadequate response of the Panel of Reference has trivialized the solemn charge from the primates and has allowed disorder to multiply unnecessarily. We recognize with regret the growing evidence that the provinces that have taken action creating the current crisis in the Communion continue moving in a direction that will result in their "walking apart." We call for urgent and serious implementation of the recommendations of the Windsor Report. Un-Scriptural and unilateral decisions, especially on moral issues, tear the fabric of our Communion and require appropriate discipline at every level to maintain our unity. While the Global South calls for the errant provinces to be disciplined, we will continue to pray for all who embrace these erroneous teachings that they will be led to repentance and restoration.

Spiritual Leadership

34. Our ongoing participation in ministry and mission requires Godly and able spiritual leadership at all times. We are encouraged that many inspirational leaders in our midst bear witness to the Scriptures and are effectively bringing the Gospel to surrounding cultures. We commit ourselves to identify the next generation of leaders and will seek to equip and deploy them wherever they are needed.

35. We need inspirational leaders and accountability structures. These mechanisms, which we are looking into, must ensure that leaders are accountable to God, to those over us in the Lord, to the flock and to one another in accordance to the Scriptures. This last aspect is in keeping with the principle of bishops and leaders acting in council. In this way, leaders become the role models that are so needed for the flock.

Youth

36. The Global South emphasizes the involvement and development of youth in the life of the Church. The youth delegates encouraged the whole gathering by the following collective

statement during the Encounter: *"Many youths in the Global South are taking up the challenge of living in moral purity in the face of the rising influence of immoral values and practice, and the widening epidemic of HIV and AIDS. Young people will be ready to give their lives to the ministry of the Church if she gives them exemplary spiritual leadership and a purpose to live for. Please pray that we will continue to be faithful as the Church of 'today and tomorrow.' It is also our heart's cry that the Communion will remain faithful to the Gospel."*

Poverty

37. As the church catholic, we share a common concern for the universal problem of debt and poverty. The inequity that exists between the rich and the poor widens as vast sums borrowed by previous governments were not used for the intended purposes. Requiring succeeding generations of people, who never benefited from the loans and resources, to repay them will impose a crushing and likely insurmountable burden. We welcome and appreciate the international efforts of debt reduction and cancellation; for example, the steps recently carried out by G8 leaders.

38. A dimension of responsible stewardship and accountability is the clear call to be financially self-sustaining. We commend the new initiative for financial self-sufficiency and development being studied by the Council of Anglican Provinces of Africa (CAPA). This is not only necessary because of the demands of human dignity; it is the only way to have sustainable economic stability.

HIV and AIDS

39. A holy Church combines purity and compassion in its witness and service. The population of the world is under assault by the HIV and AIDS pandemic, but the people of much of the Global South are hit particularly hard because of poverty, lifestyle habits, lack of teaching and the paucity

of appropriate medication. Inspired by the significant success of the Church in Uganda in tackling HIV and AIDS, all our provinces commit to learn and apply similar intentional programs that emphasize abstinence and faithfulness in marriage. We call on governments to ensure that they are providing adequate medication and treatment for those infected.

Corruption

40. The holy Church will "show forth fruits that befit repentance."[15] Many of us live in regions that have been deeply wounded by corruption. Not only do we have a responsibility to live transparent lives of utmost honesty in the Church, we are called to challenge the culture in which we live.[16] Corruption consumes the soul of society and must be challenged at all costs. Transparency and accountability are key elements that we must manifest in bearing witness to the cultures in which we live.

Violent Conflict

41. Many of us from across the Global South live juxtaposed with violent conflict, most egregiously manifest in violence against innocents. In spite of the fact that the conflicts that grip many of our provinces have resulted in many lives being lost, we are not defeated. We find hope in the midst of our pain and inspiration from the martyrs who have shed their blood. Their sacrifice calls us to faithfulness. Their witness provokes us to pursue holiness. We commit ourselves to grow to become faithful witnesses who "do not love their lives even unto death."[17]

---

15. Matthew 3:8.
16. Micah 6:8.
17. Revelation 12:11.

E. We Press On

42. We emerge from the Encounter strengthened to uphold the supreme authority of the Word of God and the doctrinal formularies that have undergirded the Anglican Communion for over four-and-a-half centuries. Communion requires alignment with the will of God first and foremost, which establishes our commonality with one another. Such expressions of the will of God which Anglicans should hold in common are: one Lord, one faith, one baptism; Holy Scripture; apostolic teaching and practice; the historic Creeds of the Christian Church; the Articles of Religion and the doctrinal tenets as contained in the 1662 *Book of Common Prayer*. Holding truth and grace together by the power of the Holy Spirit, we go forward as those entrusted "with the faith once delivered."[18]

43. By the Red Sea, God led us to renew our covenant with him. We have committed ourselves to obey him fully, to love him wholly, and to serve him in the world as a "kingdom of priests and a holy nation."[19] God also has helped us to renew our bonds of fellowship with one another, that we may "stand firm in one spirit, contending as one man in the faith of the Gospel."[20]

44. We offer to God this growing and deepening fellowship among the Global South churches that we might be a servant body to the larger Church and to the world. We see ourselves as a unifying body, moving forward collectively as servants of Christ to do what he is calling us to do both locally in our provinces and globally as the "scattered people of God throughout the world."[21]

45. Jesus Christ, "that Great Shepherd of the sheep,"[22] is caring

---

18. Jude 3.

19. Exodus 19:6.

20. Philippians 1:27.

21. 1 Peter 1:1.

22. Hebrews 13:20; Micah 5:4.

for his flock worldwide, and he is gathering into his one fold lost sheep from every tribe and nation. We continue to depend on God's grace to enable us to participate with greater vigor in Christ's great enterprise of saving love.[23] We shall press on to glorify the Father in the power of the Spirit until Christ comes again. Even so, come Lord Jesus.

---

23. 1 Peter 2:25; John 10:14-16.

CHAPTER FIVE

Anglican, Presbyterian themes similar

As differences over Christology, Biblical authority and other theological issues continue to threaten the peace, unity and purity of the Protestant mainline denominations, the two main themes permeating the "Hope and a Future" conference – "Who do you say that I am?" and "Choose you this day" – echoed themes expressed earlier in the year during Gathering IX sponsored by the Presbyterian Coalition.

At the Gathering in Orlando, Fla., Gerrit Scott Dawson said the peace, unity and purity of the Church "lies in the great resources of the Church: the gift of the Holy Spirit, the Holy Scriptures and the historic confessions."

In an appeal repeated in various ways in Pittsburgh, Dawson said that "the Church is the Creation of the Triune God, called into being and sent into the world as Father, Son and Holy Spirit to glorify one another in dynamic love."

All of us, he said, "have our life together always and only as recipients of grace that is not of our devising or deserving. We are the outworking of the divine love as it was and is expressed in the field of our humanity, in the world where we live."

The work of Dawson and Mark R. Patterson was published in a book, *Given and Sent in One Love: The True Church of Jesus Christ*, that was distributed to all Gathering IX participants. In it, Patterson is just as emphatic about the grace of God:

> "The loss of peace, unity and purity [in the Church] are inevitable wherever and whenever the church misunderstands, rejects, annuls, or redefines the grace of God made ours in Christ. Within the Catholic, Protestant and Reformed traditions, grace is the defining characteristic of both God's act on our behalf and the character of our relationship with him.

> "Grace is the singularly precise description of God's work of redemption and our response of repentance and faith," Patterson says. "Grace is a concrete reality flowing from the nature of God and manifesting itself precisely and efficaciously in the person and work of the Son. Grace, having its source in the being and will of the Father and manifesting itself in the Son, becomes, by the act of the Spirit, a transformative reality by which our relationship with God is restored and our lives redeemed."

Those who attended the "Hope and a Future" conference in Pittsburgh heard those themes repeated, with slight variations, over and over again – in sermons, addresses, hymns, question-and-answer sessions, discussions and presentations.

The Rev. Dr. Leslie P. Fairfield, a professor of church history at Trinity Episcopal School for Ministry in Ambridge, Penn., said,

"Our institutional arrangements with the Episcopal Church will take whatever shape they may. The process will be painful. But let's not get bogged down in that mess. It's a choice between morass or mission. We need to make the mental shift now, and lean into our future."

Episcopal Bishop Robert W. Duncan Jr. opened the conference by saying that "Jesus Christ is our hope. He is the whole of it. He is the sum and substance of it."

The reason for the conference, he said, is "because we need Jesus and one another more than ever. In times of storm and struggle, it is our support for one another, with God's grace, that gets us through.

"The way forward for Biblical and missionary Anglicans –
and Christians – is increasingly clear and involves all of us
together," Duncan said. "Because you have been called. No matter where you are or how insignificant you believe the contribution you have to make, come claim your part and come understand what is your hope and your future."

The Rev. Henry Luke Orombi, Primate of the Anglican
Church of Uganda, said that the people in his church answered
that call.

"We preached the Gospel, and we were not afraid," he said.
"You also must not be afraid when voices of your culture go
against you. We encourage you to be faithful. Together, we know
the way of the cross. Jesus Christ died, but he also lives, and we
are duty bound to remain faithful to that living Lord."

The Rev. Peter Jasper Akinola, Primate of all Nigeria, said
that, "The Word of God is implanted in us. We cannot hold it,
we must give it up.... We believe very strongly in the fact that he
who gave us that Word has all authority – not just on earth, but
also in heaven. He told us the imperative – go therefore and
make disciples. Jesus Christ had been given all authority – not
just power, but authority. And because we cannot but go and do
it, we must then do what he says and proclaim his Word."

The Rev. John A.M. Guernsey, dean of the Mid-Atlantic Convocation of the Anglican Communion Network, said that, "it is a
great joy and privilege to be here at this conference with so
many who know that it matters a great deal what you believe."

"In the Scriptures, hope is not some vague wishful thinking,
as in, 'I hope things work out for our Church, but they probably
won't.' No, hope is a sure expectation, a confident looking to the
future because of the victory won on the cross by Jesus, who is
called our hope."

CHAPTER SIX

Spread the faith
with a 'new Reformation'

The Rev. Rick Warren asked the participants at the first-ever international conference "Hope and a Future" to join a "new Reformation" to spread the Christian faith throughout the world.

Warren, the best-selling author of *The Purpose-Driven Life* and the pastor of Saddleback Church in California, said, "History is in the making here. You know it and I know it. I am privileged to be here to watch it."

Warren later told *The Pittsburgh Post-Gazette* that he was praying for "God to bring good out of bad" in the troubles besetting the Episcopal Church.

He expressed support for the theologically conservative participants at the conference, saying they were standing for Biblical truth, but he called for all Christians to work together despite their differences.

"It really doesn't matter what your label is. If you love Jesus, we're on the same team," he said, adding that that God uses many churches and traditions to meet broad and varied spiritual needs.

"Now I don't agree with everything in everybody's denomination, including my own. I don't agree with everything that Catholics do or Pentecostals do, but what binds us together is so much stronger than what divides us," he said.

"I really do feel that these people are brothers and sisters in God's family. I am looking to build bridges with the Orthodox Church, looking to build bridges with the Catholic Church, with the Anglican Church, and say, 'What can we do together that we have been unable to do by ourselves?'"

In his plenary address, Warren also urged the participants to use the resources of "the universal, worldwide church of Jesus Christ in all of its local expressions" to help the poorest of the poor.

Warren said he had completely missed the importance that the Bible places on the care of the poor until after his book became a bestseller and he asked God what to do with the money it generated. That's when he learned about the importance of caring for the poorest of the poor, Warren said.

"How did I miss this thing on poverty?" he asked. "I went to Bible school and seminary and got a doctorate. How did I miss 2,000 verses in the Bible?"

CHAPTER SEVEN

'Hope stands on the Word'

"Hope stands on the Word of God, springs from intimacy with the Lord and arises out of suffering for Jesus," the Rev. John A.M. Guernsey told participants at the conference.

He began by reminding his audience that, at the Global Conference on the Decade of Evangelism 10 years ago, "when mission leaders from throughout the Anglican Communion gathered to report on their progress in spreading the Gospel or, in the case of the Episcopal Church, our sad lack thereof, George Carey, then Archbishop of Canterbury, lamented some forms of Anglicanism, which he called, 'it doesn't matter what you believe as long as you don't believe it too strongly.'"

"It is a great joy and privilege to be here at this conference with so many who know that it matters a great deal what you believe," Guernsey said, "and who – thanks be to God – believe it with such great passion."

"In the Scriptures, hope is not some vague wishful thinking, as in, 'I hope things work out for our Church, but they probably won't.' No, hope is a sure expectation, a confident looking to the future because of the victory won on the cross by Jesus, who is called our hope."

First, Guernsey said, hope stands on the Word of God.

"Everyone who hears these words of mine and puts them into practice," Jesus said, "is like a wise man who built his house on the rock. The rain came down, the streams rose, and the winds blew and beat against that house; yet it did not fall, because it had its foundation on the rock."

The crisis in the Episcopal Church (USA), Guernsey said, "is not at its root about human sexuality, though that is certainly the flash point that has attracted so much of the attention. It is about the authority and interpretation of Holy Scripture. Not only have the un-Biblical actions of the General Convention and many dioceses approved what God has forbidden, but the explicit statements of all too many bishops have denied the truth and authority of the Word of God."

"The presiding bishop once said, 'Broadly speaking, the Episcopal Church is in conflict with Scripture ... The mind of Christ operative in the church over time ... has led the church, in effect, to contradict the words of the Gospel.'

"That is a grievously false statement," Guernsey said. "Of course, the Episcopal Church is in conflict with Scripture. But the idea that the mind of Christ would contradict 'the words of the Gospel' is not only wrong, it is dangerous. We are not free to make up our own religion, our own version of truth, and then arrogantly declare that it is the mind of Christ. The rejection of the authority of Scripture has put the Episcopal Church, like the house of the foolish man, on a foundation of sand, and we see the resulting cracks and crumbling all around us.

"Still another prominent bishop said this: 'We believe God didn't stop revealing God's self when the canon of Scripture was closed. We worship a living God, not one who checked out 2,000 years ago.' But that's a false dichotomy. God hasn't stopped revealing himself, but he will never contradict what he has revealed in Scripture."

He said another bishop said, "The church wrote the Bible and we can rewrite it,' and another bishop said, 'Jesus changed the Old Testament and he gave us that power. Now we can change the New Testament in like manner.'"

"But we are not to judge the truth of Scripture," Guernsey said. "The truth of Scripture judges us! It was J.B. Phillips, I believe, who likened Bible translation to rewiring a house with the power left on. The Word of God is living and active and we manipulate it at our peril."

Then, quoting Jeremiah 8:8, 9b, Guernsey said, "How can you say, 'We are wise, for we have the law of the Lord,' when actually the lying pen of the scribes has handled it falsely ... Since they have rejected the Word of the Lord, what kind of wisdom do they have?"

Second, he said, hope springs from "intimacy with the Lord."

Jeremiah 29:11 contains "the famous verse, which is the basis for our conference theme, 'For I know the plans I have for you,' declares the Lord, 'plans to prosper you and not to harm you, plans to give you hope and a future.'"

That promise, Guernsey warned, is linked "directly to faithful, wholehearted seeking of the Lord in prayer. Verse 11 is followed by these words: 'Then you will call upon me and come and pray to me, and I will listen to you. You will seek me and find me when you seek me with all your heart.'"

"It's important to remember that Jeremiah's words were spoken in a time of great suffering, when the people of Jerusalem had been exiled to Babylon. They had lost their homes and their nation, but even more horrific, they had lost the Temple, their place of worship. They were tempted to despair, to hopelessness.

"The antidote to this discouragement, Jeremiah told them, was to be found in the intimacy of prayer. It is a remedy we find again and again in the Scriptures," he said.

Guernsey then talked about David in Psalm 27. David cried out at the relentless assaults of his enemies, but trusted in the Lord: "'Though an army besiege me, my heart will not fear; though war break out against me, even then will I be confident.' Why? Where did this hope come from? David makes it clear in the very next verse: 'One thing I ask of the Lord, this is what I seek: that I may dwell in the house of the Lord all the days of my life, to gaze upon the beauty of the Lord and to seek him in his temple.'"

"It was this intimacy with the Lord," Guernsey said, "born out of intense encounters in worship and in prayer, that sustained David when he was under assault. Hope overflowed out of his life of prayer. I suspect that most Christians, certainly most evangelical and catholic Christians, would agree that intimacy with the Lord is a good thing. In fact, I know a great many people who are open to a deeper prayer life, a closer relationship with the Lord.

"Well, at this point in my life, I am open to losing a little weight, too, but I am not really committed to it," he said. "Do you understand the difference? I know many who are open to a deeper devotional life. They would be delighted if they woke up one morning and found that they knew God more closely, heard his voice more clearly. But they are not committed to it. They are not passionate about the things of God. They are not seeking him with all their heart, but it is in intimate communion with the Lord that we find hope.

"If we are to be people of hope, we must set aside every other demand, every other opportunity, until we have come first into that secret place of intimacy with the Lord. It was the great teacher on prayer, Dr. A.J. Gordon, who said, 'You can do more than pray after you have prayed, but you cannot do more than pray until you have prayed.'"

Third, Guernsey said, hope arises out of "suffering for Jesus."

In Romans 5, Paul said, "We also rejoice in our sufferings, because we know that suffering produces perseverance; perseverance, character; and character, hope."

When Paul speaks of suffering, Guernsey said, "he is referring to suffering for the sake of Christ. While a bad back or an obnoxious brother-in-law may be a form of suffering, it is not what the apostle had in mind. We are to celebrate when we suffer for the name of Jesus. 'Rejoice and be glad,' Jesus himself said, 'because great is your reward in heaven.'"[1]

"But the reward is not automatic," he said. "Suffering is a test. We are being tested and proved. How we respond to suffering for Jesus is the key. Suffering produces perseverance, Paul says, or endurance, as some translations have it. You can't develop endurance without suffering because there must be

---

1. Matthew 5:12.

something for you to endure. You can't develop a virtue without having the circumstances to exercise that virtue. You can't become a patient person without being forced to wait. You cannot become merciful without being wounded and needing to forgive. And you can't form perseverance without the experience of suffering for Christ.

"How we respond to the pressures we are facing matters for the cause of Christ, now and for eternity," he said. "We will one day be judged not only for what we have done, but also for who we have become through our afflictions. Suffering is a test. If we face criticism and ridicule of our Biblical faith and we fall silent, we fail the test. If we face the loss of property or career or reputation and shrink back, we are not worthy of Christ."

Yet, Guernsey said, "God intends suffering for our good and for the extension of his Kingdom. Have you come to that place of maturity in Christ where you can echo these words of Psalm 119: 'It was good for me to be afflicted so that I might learn your decrees.' Or these words of Isaiah: 'I will walk humbly all my years because of this anguish of my soul ... Surely it was for my benefit that I suffered such anguish."

Talking about the present state of the denomination, he said that it has taken "this crisis to humble us. By God's grace, our need has driven us back to Jesus. Our desperation is bringing us back to the Lord, and for this we must give thanks. If we will respond rightly to the attacks we are experiencing, then God will use them for our good."

"If we react to suffering with bitterness, resentment, anger, hostility, vengeance, then we forfeit the blessing, our witness is compromised, and we prove ourselves unworthy of the reward that would be ours in Christ. But if we meet hostility and attack with grace and forgiveness and with the steadfast proclamation of the Gospel, then God will bring us through to glory," Guernsey said, adding:

"Jesus is our hope. His Word is our sure foundation. Intimacy with him is our deepest joy. Suffering for him, our great privilege. 'To him who sits on the throne and to the Lamb be praise and honor and glory and power, for ever and ever!'"

CHAPTER EIGHT

Church of the martyrs and missionaries

The Church of the martyrs and of missionaries was the message from two African primates, recently honored for "exemplary fidelity to the authority of Scripture and exceptional pastoral courage in their efforts to restore the prophetic voice of the Church as the moral conscience of culture."

The Rev. Henry Luke Orombi, Primate of the Anglican Church of Uganda, said that "the church in Uganda is a very small church, in a very small country, and I'm coming here to share a very small story about a very big God."

Orombi was born in Goli, Uganda, in 1949. A graduate of St. John's College at Nottingham University in the United Kingdom, he became bishop of Nebbi in 1993 and archbishop of Uganda in 2004.

He talked about his country during the Victorian era, and how the people of that time "invited missionaries, and they came and began to plant the Gospel seed in our nation."

"Our church began to see the blood of the martyrs from infancy," Orombi said. "That, of course, brought about the growth of the church. The church of Uganda will not say yes to sin, even if we are persecuted for it. We understand persecution because our church is the product of fire. On the shores of Lake

Victoria, a tribal king fed our young men to the fire because they would not succumb to his sexual advances. These men believed King Jesus was more powerful than the king of Uganda. Every June 3rd, we remember them for standing firm in the Gospel."

"Then," Orombi said, "we were tested again when we faced persecution under Idi Amin from 1971 to 1979. Our highest leadership was murdered under the rule of Amin. The blood of the martyrs is the seed of the Gospel."

He spoke about when he was preaching in Entebbe and his group "was rounded up by the secret police and locked up." Describing the brutal conditions in the prison, he said their "eyes were opened to atrocities and the depths our country had sunk to."

Orombi also spoke about how the secret police entered the home of the archbishop looking for guns and how the archbishop "paid a price for the Gospel." He didn't have any guns, Orombi said, but he "picked up a Bible and told the secret police, 'The Bible is my gun.'"

"We preached the Gospel, and we were not afraid," he said. "You also must not be afraid when voices of your culture go against you. We encourage you to be faithful. Together, we know the way of the cross. Jesus Christ died, but he also lives, and we are duty bound to remain faithful to that living Lord."

In 2004, Orombi faced a crisis on a different front, as the Episcopal Church (USA) defied Biblical faith by enthroning as bishop a man who had left his wife and children to enter a homosexual partnership. Orombi publicly opposed this action, severed relations with the "apostate" Episcopal Church, refused to take communion with Episcopal President Frank Griswold, and declined to accept any mission money from the U.S. denomination.

Later, when the pastors of three Episcopal churches in California were disciplined for refusing to obey their liberal bishop, Orombi asked one of his bishops to give oversight to the California priests. This "invasion" provoked an uproar from the Episcopal establishment.

"We are committed to those of the Episcopal Church (USA) who are committed to Scripture and love Jesus Christ as Lord," Orombi said at the time. "For us in Uganda, we say this without fear."

In Pittsburgh, he told the crowd that, "You in America will have to suffer because the Gospel is not a pleasant message for everybody. But you are not in isolation. Remember that we are into the people's business. It is the people's ministry – feed them, tend them, take care of them."

"Move away from self-pity," Orombi said. "Move away from too much talking – the talking is over. The church in Africa was talking while Islam was advancing, arguing while Islam was advancing. We almost lost the Church. But you can never lose the Church while Christ is alive.

"We come to stand with you," he said. "We are here to encourage you. Brothers and sisters, fix your eyes on Jesus Christ and he will make it possible. Trust in the Lord. It may be hard now, but trust in the Lord. Without him, you can do nothing."

The second speaker from Africa was the Rev. Peter Jasper Akinola, Primate of all Nigeria, who has been fearless in criticizing the Episcopal Church (USA) and the Archbishop of Canterbury over what he has called their failure to uphold the Church's historic stand on sexual morality.

Akinola was born in Nigeria in 1944. Having earned the highest theological diploma with distinction from the Theological College of Northern Nigeria, he came to the United States and earned his master's degree in theological studies from Virginia Theological Seminary, which later awarded him a Doctor of Divinity degree.

Returning to Nigeria in 1989, he was consecrated a bishop and proceeded to build his Abuja Diocese into prosperous self-reliance with investments in the hospitality industry and in the Nigerian money market. Within his diocese, he established 12 nursery/primary schools and two secondary schools. In 2000, Akinola was elected primate and metropolitan of All Nigeria, and began moving his denomination toward self-reliance.

Appointed as the chairman of the Global South in 2002 and chairman of the Conference of Anglican Provinces in Africa in 2003, Akinola has emerged as a leading spokesman for Biblical orthodoxy in the midst of the Anglican Communion's theological crises. He has been fearless in contending with Griswold and Rowan Williams, the Archbishop of Canterbury, over their failure to uphold the Church's historic stand on sexual morality.

Using as his text Jeremiah 1:9, "Then the Lord put forth his hand, and touched my mouth. And the Lord said unto me, Behold, I have put my words in thy mouth," Akinola said that, "The Word of God is implanted in us. We cannot hold it, we must give it up."

"That is why," he said, "we see ourselves as a missionary church. We believe very strongly in the fact that He who gave us that Word has all authority – not just on earth, but also in heaven. He told us the imperative – go therefore and make disciples. Jesus Christ had been given all authority – not just power, but authority. And, because we cannot but go and do it, we must then do what he says and proclaim his Word."

Akinola talked about how, in just 16 years, the Anglican Church of Nigeria has grown from one diocese to three, and the growth continues.

"To be a missionary church is non-negotiable," he said. "There is no alternative. You must proclaim the Gospel. We are not missionaries to ourselves alone, but also in the Congo, training workers for the church in Sudan, sending missionaries to Madagascar and seeking avenues to reach out to other parts of the Global South.

"Jesus Christ calls on us to do his will," Akinola said. "How long are you going to continue to waver? How long are you going to continue to doubt?

"This is the moment to make a decision," he said. "The Word of God is the supreme rule of life and living. What we [in Nigeria] have done has freed us. Today, we are free. As long as we hold this [Word of God] together, we are with you every inch of the way."

Both men, and two others, were honored last fall by *Kairos*

Journal, an online resource for pastors and church leaders that is received by readers in more than 80 countries.

The award gives international recognition to people who demonstrate "exemplary fidelity to the authority of Scripture and exceptional pastoral courage in their efforts to restore the prophetic voice of the Church as the moral conscience of culture."

The four Anglican recipients of the *Kairos Journal* award were: Orombi; Akinola; Datuk Young Ping Chung, archbishop of the Province of South East Asia; and Gregory Venables, archbishop of the Southern Cone of America.

CHAPTER NINE

Property issues hover in background

As in the Presbyterian Church (USA), the United Methodist Church and other denominations in the Protestant mainline, property issues – though only alluded to by the speakers in Pittsburgh – hovered in the background of the first-ever international conference "Hope and a Future."

As court cases pop up all over the country over who owns a congregation's property, the Presbyterian Church (USA) has begun sending teams to meet with synod and presbytery representatives to ensure that "church corporation articles ... state clearly that the church property is held in trust" for the denomination.

At least two property-dispute cases at this writing are under way in civil courts involving Presbyterian Church (USA) congregations. Both congregations, which are evangelical and orthodox, voted to leave the PCUSA because of their disagreement with the actions and decisions of denominational leaders.

In California, Serone Church, an independent Korean congregation in Artesia, is trying to stop the Presbytery of Hamni's attempt to seize its property and assets. In North Carolina, Hephzibah Evangelical Church near Bessemer City has asked the North Carolina Court of Appeals to reverse a ruling by a state judge, who awarded the property to the presbytery.

Both congregations are challenging the PCUSA's property trust clause, G-8.0201, in the *Book of Order*, which states:

> "All property held by or for a particular church, a presbytery, a synod, the General Assembly, or the Presbyterian Church (USA), whether legal title is lodged in a corporation, a trustee or trustees, or an unincorporated association, and whether the property is used in programs of a particular church or of a more inclusive governing body or retained for the production of income, is held in trust nevertheless for the use and benefit of the Presbyterian Church (USA)."

Another case involved St. Luke's United Methodist Church, a congregation in Fresno, Calif., that left that 8.5-million denomination in 2000 to become an independent Methodist church.

In December 2004, the California Supreme Court let stand a lower court's ruling that the congregation had the right to revoke the United Methodist property trust agreement and keep its property. That same year, a Maryland state court ruled in favor of a dissident congregation that left the AME Zion Church.

Similar challenges of church property laws are being pursued by congregations in the Episcopal Church (USA) and, in response, the Anglican Communion Network has established a legal hotline with a team of six lawyers on call.

In October 2005, the Episcopal Church's Property Disputes Steering Committee held a conference call among 32 participants, including 28 bishops and Presiding Bishop Frank Griswold and his attorney, Virtue Online reported.

The meeting, Virtue Online reported, was an outgrowth of a Property Task Force "with legal overtones" set up by the bishops at their recent meeting in Puerto Rico, which was described as "an ominous admission that the Episcopal Church might come apart at the seams with millions of dollars being spent on lawsuits over divided and fleeing parishes who believe that the Episcopal Church has abandoned the historic Christian faith."

The 10-member task force of attorneys and other experts was created, Virtue Online reported, "to help defend the Episcopal

Church and its dioceses against attempts by congregations or other dioceses to secede from the Episcopal Church with their property."

Nineteen bishops from both sides in the issue met in July 2005 in Los Angeles to discuss ways to divide assets, *The Washington Times* reported. Although Bishop John B. Chane of Washington threatened a walkout if anyone divulged what was discussed, Bishop V. Gene Robinson – who had left his wife and children to enter a homosexual partnership and whose elevation to bishop sparked outrage throughout the denomination – revealed details about the gathering in a Sept. 23 interview with The Associated Press. *The Living Church* reported that several bishops were "livid" about Robinson's disclosures.

At stake in the Episcopalian dispute are millions, if not billions, of dollars in real estate, endowments, pension funds and investments involved in a denomination founded in 1789.

Wicks Stephens, a litigation and trial attorney from Los Angeles, heads up the legal team for the Anglican Communion Network. Stephens told *The Washington Times* that he has been asked to advise on "dozens" of conflicts nationwide.

"Our biggest challenge at the moment is that too many bishops are looking to the canons [ecclesiastical laws] rather than being pastors to people who don't agree with them," he said. "If there's a desire to amicably deal with issues of disagreement, we're not seeing very much from the opposition in that respect."

Although some state courts have upheld denominational property trust clauses, the recent rulings by appellate courts in Maryland and California concluded otherwise. Those appellate court rulings held that local congregations that had voted to leave their denominations could retain their property because they either never agreed to place the property in trust or, if the property were subject to trust, the trust was revocable. They said congregations that decided by majority vote to leave their denominations could rescind their submission to a trust clause adopted by the denomination.

Since 1979, rulings by the U.S. Supreme Court increasingly have emphasized that church property rules must be resolved by a "neutral principles of law" analysis.

In *Jones v. Wolf* (1979), the court declared:

"The primary advantages of the neutral-principles approach are that it is completely secular in operation, and yet flexible enough to accommodate all forms of religious organization and polity. The method relies exclusively on objective, well-established concepts of trust and property law familiar to lawyers and judges. It thereby promises to free civil courts completely from entanglement in questions of religious doctrine, polity, and practice."

The court added:

"As a means of adjudicating a church property dispute, a State is constitutionally entitled to adopt a 'neutral principles of law' analysis involving consideration of the deeds, state statutes governing the holding of church property, the local church's charter, and the general church's constitution."

CHAPTER TEN

'Voices that are speaking for division'

While participants were celebrating "the rebirth of a Biblical, missionary and united Anglicanism" in Pittsburgh, the gay bishop whose consecration in 2003 set off seismic shocks in the worldwide Anglican Communion was criticizing one of the Pennsylvania event's featured speakers as one of "the voices that are speaking for division."

The Rev. Peter Jasper Akinola, primate of all Nigeria, has been fearless in criticizing the Episcopal Church (USA) and the Archbishop of Canterbury over what he has called their failure to uphold the Church's historic stand on sexual morality. Akinola was one of the main speakers at the first-ever international conference "Hope and a Future."

It was sponsored by the Anglican Communion Network, created by conservative bishops after the denomination consecrated a gay man, V. Gene Robinson, as bishop of New Hampshire and gave tacit approval to same-sex blessings.

The Rev. Dr. Leslie P. Fairfield, a professor of church history at Trinity Episcopal School for Ministry in Ambridge, Penn., said those and other changes within the Episcopal Church had made it "a non-Christian religion" and its leadership had "embraced a foreign, alien and pagan religion."

Conservatives, said the Rev. Dr. Kendall Harmon, canon theologian of the Diocese of South Carolina, are in a battle "for the soul of the Western Church. It's a battle for the shape of Christianity in the whole world."

The Church Times in London reported that Robinson said primates such as those who spoke in Pittsburgh do not necessarily speak for their provinces.

"It's a fallacy to assume that Peter Akinola speaks for the communion," he said. "Will a listening process change Peter Akinola's mind about this issue? Probably not.

"It's no surprise to me that Peter Akinola has trouble comprehending the context in which we find ourselves in America," Robinson told the newspaper. "To be a homosexual in Nigeria is to be arrested and imprisoned, so how would Peter ever have the opportunity to meet a faithful and loyal and prayerful Anglican who also happens to be gay or lesbian, and get to know them and have his heart changed by that?"

Robinson was in London to participate in the tenth anniversary of Changing Attitude, an advocacy organization that seeks full affirmation for gay and lesbians in the Anglican Church.

Restrictions had been imposed on his visit, said the Rev. Nicholas Holtam, vicar of St Martin-in-the-Fields. He said it was important that "we keep to the ground rules," as agreed with the Bishop of London and the Archbishop of Canterbury. "Bishop Robinson will be one among us during the service and will speak afterward," he told *The Church Times*.

During the London visit, Robinson met informally with Rowan Williams, the Archbishop of Canterbury. The newspaper reported that the meeting was part of Williams' commitment to listening to all sides of the debate in the Anglican Communion about homosexuality. No details of the meeting were released.

Robinson told *The Church Times* he has no doubt that the danger facing the Anglican Communion is serious and deep, but he does not believe that the Episcopal Church (USA) is heading toward "an inevitable train wreck."

"We are irreconcilable only if we choose to be," he said. "Reconciliation is the ministry we are all called to, and so to declare ourselves out of communion with one another is simply an infraction against God."

The rest of the world, Robinson said, does not understand how the American denomination works. "In our polity, the church speaks only when the laity, the clergy, and the bishops speak at the General Convention. It's what makes our church so very different from the provinces of the Anglican Communion."

Asked if he would he have done anything differently, Robinson said, "It's very difficult to say. On the one hand, we have learned that to make such a momentous decision without more consultation was perhaps inappropriate on our part. But you have to understand that consultation could not have happened until I was elected, and no one knew I was going to be elected. Being nominated is easy; being elected is hard."

"All I can tell you," he said, "is that the General Convention prayerfully and thoughtfully considered this and agonized over it. It was not some flippant or mindless or prayer-less action."

He told *The Church Times* that he could be wrong and maybe should not even be speculating, but his personal view is that he does not see the American denomination moving backward.

"I can't be unmade a bishop," Robinson said. "We will continue to nourish these relationships around the globe, and trust that the Communion that is there will actually win over the voices that are speaking for division."

CHAPTER ELEVEN

'Neo-Puritan'
fundamentalists criticized

Conservative Episcopalians seeking "the rebirth of a Biblical, missionary and united Anglicanism" are being lam-
basted by their critics as "neo-Puritan" Protestant funda-
mentalists and "the voices that are speaking for division."

Some of the participants at the first-ever international conference "Hope and a Future" included members of the clergy, who
had lost their pastoral licenses, and parishioners, who faced losing buildings, in theological disputes with more liberal bishops
in the United States.

The organizer of the conference, Bishop Robert W. Duncan
Jr. of Pittsburgh, said he expects liberal activists in the denomination to attempt to depose him as bishop, noting that one
national network already had called for such action.

Duncan, in an interview with *The Pittsburgh Post-Gazette*,
said, "I'm not planning to go anywhere, but I think they will try
to remove me. That is going to be my Good Friday. That is going
to be my people's Good Friday. But I think we are prepared. We
will not turn away from Jesus."

Throughout the conference, leaders spoke of a "realignment"
of worldwide Anglicanism. Drawing on a Bible passage in
which Joshua challenged the Israelites to choose between the
true God and pagan gods, there was a running theme of "choose

you this day."[1]

Duncan, though, told the newspaper that he could not define that choice in institutional terms. No matter what church people belong to, he said, "the choice is for Jesus, as opposed to something less or a counterfeit. And we really think that [counterfeit] is what is being offered by the Episcopal Church at the moment."

Supporters of the denomination's present policy on gays, including the gay bishop whose consecration in 2003 set off seismic shocks in the worldwide Anglican Communion, ratcheted up their criticism of Duncan and his supporters.

V. Gene Robinson, the only gay bishop in the Episcopal Church (USA), told *The Church Times* in London that he does not believe that the Episcopal Church USA is heading toward "an inevitable train wreck."

"We are irreconcilable only if we choose to be," he said. "Reconciliation is the ministry we are all called to, and so to declare ourselves out of communion with one another is simply an infraction against God.

"I can't be unmade a bishop," Robinson said. "We will continue to nourish these relationships around the globe, and trust that the Communion that is there will actually win over the voices that are speaking for division."

Lionel Demiel, president of Progressive Episcopalians of Pittsburgh, said remarks by Duncan and other primates at the conference "could be read as an invitation to leave" the denomination.

"We basically have a long history of working things out," Deimel said, "but this is the most serious thing to happen to the Episcopal Church, and it has mobilized people on both sides."

"My preference is that we all stand together and work out our differences and, in some cases, accept our differences," he said.

After the consecration of Robinson, Demiel, in a letter to Rowan Williams, the archbishop of Canterbury, said that the American Anglican Council and the Anglican Communion Net-

---

1. Joshua 24:15.

work "began to implement its plan to take over the Episcopal Church. Any objective analysis of the situation can only conclude that, having failed in this and previous attempts to move this mainline church sharply to the right through democratic means, a group of Episcopal bishops has decided to stage a coup d'état."

In his letter, Demiel said "the inclusive nature of the Episcopal Church is now threatened by a small dissident group of its bishops who arrogantly assert special knowledge of God's truth and demand that their opinions prevail, even though those opinions have been expressly rejected in scrupulously fair and regular votes by General Convention."

Continually calling the theologically conservative bishops dissidents, Demiel said that they have "repeatedly failed to assert successfully their narrow view of scripture and revelation. They have increasingly turned to both ecclesiastical and secular courts in their quest for power, and they now seek to employ the Anglican Communion, not in its traditional collegial and advisory role, but as a weapon to be wielded against their theological opponents. In this plan, they have naïvely joined forces with domestic political reactionaries whose goal is to remove people of faith from the discussion in the public square of issues of social, economic, and environmental justice; and they have curried favor with foreign prelates and archbishops who, for their own reasons, have encouraged these bishops in their heedless rush to schism."

The Rev. Jan Nunley, a spokeswoman for the denomination, told *The Washington Times* that the tensions voiced at the Pittsburgh conference were not new.

"We're trying not to get ahead of events. We sit, watch and trust God, and hope for the spirit of reconciliation," she said.

CHAPTER TWELVE

'Road out is a one-way street'

"The road out of the Episcopal Church (USA) is a one-way street," the Rev. Canon David C. Anderson told participants at the first-ever international conference "Hope and a Future." "No one seems to be going in the opposite direction," he said. "Once people are out, they are free."

That, in a nutshell, was one of the themes prevalent during the conference, which organizers said focuses on the renewal of North American Anglicanism and "the rebirth of a Biblical, missionary and united Anglicanism."

The Anglican Communion Network, which sponsored the conference, was created by conservative bishops after the denomination's decision in 2003 to accept an openly gay bishop and give tacit approval to same-sex blessings. Since then, there have been signs of fragmentation of the denomination.

Anderson, president of the American Anglican Council and secretary of the Anglican Communion Network, said that, "in looking at the largest strategic picture, if you are in the Episcopal Church (USA) and you can stay in at least for now, try and stay and work for us because every soldier who leaves the Episcopal Church (USA) field of battle is not available to us to continue the battle. Stay as long as you can. However, when the time comes when you feel time to leave, we stand with you to work on a means of strategy to make an exit."

He said the major task facing the American Anglican Council

and the Anglican Communion Network, as well as everyone in
the hall, "is the upcoming General Conference – to call the Episcopal Church (USA) to the question, 'Choose you this day.'[1]
That is the issue for General Convention. Walk with the Anglican Communion or walk apart. Make up your mind."

His comment was greeted with thunderous applause from the
convention hall.

"We have entered a pivotal area of realignment," Anderson
said. It is a "spiritual battle for the soul of the church."

He then talked about the progress that has been made since
the network was organized in January 2004 – progress, he said
that "successfully birthed the network."

The two-year-old movement now is comprised of 10 Episcopal dioceses – Albany, Central Florida, Dallas, Fort Worth, Pittsburgh, Quincy, Rio Grande, San Joaquin, South Carolina and
Springfield – and more than 800 parishes, constituting about 10
percent of the Episcopal Church's 2.3 million members.

Anderson briefly went over why the organization was formed.
In a series of questions and answers posted on the network's
Web site, more details are provided to some of the reasons for
the formation of the organization:

**Why is ACN necessary and why should dioceses or parishes
affiliate with it?**

Following the egregious decisions made at General Convention 2003 in which the Episcopal Church abandoned 2,000 years
of Biblical teaching and historical Church order, there was a dis-
connect between the beliefs of the Episcopal Church and the
worldwide Anglican Communion. As a result, 21 provinces have
declared either impaired or broken communion with the Episcopal Church (USA), and 14 primates have recognized the ACN as
the legitimate Anglican presence in North America. The ACN,
therefore, provides a means for remaining connected with the
Anglican Communion. At a time when Church leadership is failing, ACN will provide a way for dioceses and parishes to remain

---

1.   Joshua 24:15.

under orthodox leadership.

What is the distinction between the American Anglican Council and ACN, and what role does the AAC play in the ACN?

ACN is an ecclesial body, whereas the American Anglican Council is an advocacy organization dedicated to reforming the Episcopal Church. While they share a dedication to Biblical authority, the Great Commission and the historic faith and order of Anglicanism, the two are separate entities. ACN is a link for dioceses and parishes. The AAC is an advocate for renewal of the Episcopal Church.

How is ACN a "missionary" organization?

As the Structural Charter explicitly states, the first and foremost goal of the ACN is to spread the Gospel of Jesus Christ and to carry out the mission of the Great Commission. ACN will work to bring into fellowship, with each other and with the Anglican Communion, "those who have left the Episcopal Church (USA) and those who wish to explore the tradition and worship of Anglican orthodoxy." Clergy and laity alike will be sent into often unwelcoming territory to offer orthodox leadership and the truth of the Gospel to those who are isolated or lost. New congregations, partnered with the ACN, are being formed regularly. ACN also will continue to build its relationship with Anglican Global Mission Partners, which serves as its missionary arm.

Why affiliate with the ACN?

Affiliation with ACN gathers dioceses and congregations as a true and legitimate expression of Anglicanism. Affiliation with ACN restores communion with the majority of the Anglican Communion who have severed ties with the Episcopal Church (USA). Affiliation with ACN allows dioceses, parishes and individual clergy to stand in solidarity upholding 2,000 years of Christian teaching, as well as Anglican faith and order.

Fourteen primates from around the world, the leaders of more than 45 million people – well over half of the world's Anglicans – have backed the network. The complete text of their letter of endorsement is as follows:

We, Primates of the Global South, greet you in the name of our Triune God, Father, Son, and Holy Spirit.

The actions of the Episcopal Church (USA) in the election, confirmation and consecration of Canon Gene Robinson have created a situation of grave concern for the entire Anglican Communion and beyond. Their actions are a direct repudiation of the clear teaching of the Holy Scriptures, historic faith and order of the church.

They also constitute a clear defiance of the primates of the Communion, who warned at their October meeting:

> If his consecration proceeds, we recognize that we have reached a crucial and critical point in the life of the Anglican Communion and we have had to conclude that the future of the Communion itself will be put in jeopardy. In this case, the ministry of this one bishop will not be recognized by most of the Anglican world, and many provinces are likely to consider themselves to be out of Communion with the Episcopal Church (USA).

This will tear the fabric of our Communion at its deepest level, and may lead to further division on this and further issues as provinces have to decide in consequence whether they can remain in communion with provinces that choose not to break communion with the Episcopal Church (USA).

The world needs to know that the rebellious and erroneous actions of the Episcopal Church (USA) are contrary to the teaching of the Anglican Communion and represent a departure from five thousand years of Judeo-Christian teaching and practice. By their actions, the Episcopal Church (USA) has separated itself from the remainder of the Anglican Communion and the wider Christian family.

We appeal to all the faithful to be diligent in prayer and faith and call upon Anglicans across the communion to engage in loyal witness to the risen Christ, and to resist and confront the false teaching undergirding these actions and which is leading people away from the redeeming love of Jesus into error and danger.

We ask you to join in our repentance for failing to be sufficiently forthright in adequately addressing this issue in the past, and we invite you to stand with us in a renewed struggle to uphold the received truth found in Jesus and his Word.

We reaffirm our solidarity with faithful bishops, clergy and church members in North America who remain committed the historic faith and order of the church and have rejected un-Biblical innovation. We offer our support and the full weight of our ministries and offices to those who are gathering in a 'Network of Confessing Dioceses and Congregations' now being organized in North America. We regard this network as a hopeful sign of a faithful Anglican future in North America. We invite those who are committed to the preservation of historic Biblical faith and order to join that work and its essential commitment to the Gospel.

Finally, we appeal to you to sustain us in prayer, and to intercede especially for Anglicans in North America.

'Now to him who is able to do far more abundantly beyond
all that we ask or think, according to the power that works
within us, to him be the glory in the church and in Christ
Jesus to all generations forever and ever. Amen.'[2]

Signed:

Rev. Peter Akinola, Nigeria; Rev. Drexel Gomez, West Indies; Rev. Greg Venables, Southern Cone; Rev. Joseph Marona, Sudan; Rev. Benjamin Nzimbi, Kenya; Rev. Livingstone Nkoyoyo, Uganda (retiring); Rev. Henry Orombi, Uganda; Rev. Fidele Dirokpa, Congo; Rev. Donald Mtetemela, Tanzania; Rev. Bernard Malango, Central Africa; Rev. K.J. Samuel, South India; Rev. Alexander Malik, Pakistan; Rev. Yong Ping Chung, South East Asia; and Rev. Ignacio Soliba, Philippines.

---

2. Ephesians 3:20-21.

CHAPTER THIRTEEN

'We will stand with you'

An international panel of Anglican bishops, building on a theme from the day before, told a gathering of conservative Anglicans that they would "stand with you" should their American counterparts decide to leave the Episcopal Church (USA).

"Yes, we will stand with you as long as you remain faithful, Biblical, evangelical and orthodox," said Bishop Datuk Yong Ping Chung, who represents the Province of South East Asia.

The comments from the primates from the geographic area known as the Global South came during the first-ever international conference "Hope and a Future," sponsored by the Anglican Communion Network. The two-year-old network is made up of 10 Episcopal dioceses and more than 800 parishes, constituting about 10 percent of the Episcopal Church USA's 2.3 million members.

At least 10 provinces, including those of the seven archbishops who attended the "Hope and A Future" conference, and as many as 22 of the Anglican Communion's 38 provinces, have either broken with or declared impaired relations with the 2.3-million-member Episcopal Church over its consecration of Bishop V. Gene Robinson.

Episcopal Bishop Robert W. Duncan Jr., one of the founders of the network, opened the conference by saying that it will focus on the renewal of North American Anglicanism and "the rebirth of a Biblical, missionary and united Anglicanism."

That focus is opposed to what he called "a wayward American church," whose "departures are a symptom of a deeper problem, which is the diminution of the authority of Holy Scripture."

The Rev. Peter Jasper Akinola, primate of all Nigeria, which is home to more than 18 million Anglicans, told the more than 2,000 participants that, "Jesus Christ calls on us to do his will. How long are you going to continue to waver? How long are you going to continue to doubt?"

"This is the moment to make a decision," he said. "The Word of God is the supreme rule of life and living. What we [in Nigeria] have done has freed us. Today we are free. As long as we hold this [Word of God] together, we are with you every inch of the way."

Akinola also said that, "Bishops of the network must realize time that is no longer on their side – this is your *kairos* moment to make up your mind what to do. Many of you have one leg in [the Episcopal Church] and one leg in the network. If you really want the Global South to partner with you, you must let us know exactly where you stand. Are you Episcopalian or are you network?"

The Rev. Henry Luke Orombi, primate of the Anglican Church of Uganda, had told the gathering that, "We come to stand with you. We are here to encourage you. Brothers and sisters, fix your eyes on Jesus Christ and he will make it possible."

"Trust in the Lord," he said. "It may be hard now, but trust in the Lord. Without him, you can do nothing."

Bishop Robinson Cavalcanti of Recife, Brazil, who was removed by his own archbishop for siding with American conservatives, told the audience that they were "my partners in martyrdom."

Comparing the leaders of the Episcopal Church (USA) with those guarding the tomb of Jesus after the resurrection, he said that, "In the deep of their souls, they are afraid, they are shaking. They know that, spiritually, they are like dead men."

"Don't be afraid of your bishop," Cavalcanti said. "Don't be afraid of losing your jobs, of losing your salaries. Many times the law of men needs to be broken so the law of God is obeyed."

While encouraging those in the convention hall, the primates also intensified their warnings about the possibility of a schism in the Anglican Communion if the Episcopal Church (USA) did not renounce the consecration of a gay bishop and the blessing of same-sex unions.

"There's no way for these two conflicted faiths to live under the same roof," Duncan said.

Echoing Duncan's and warnings from other Episcopal and Anglican conservatives, the primates said a break was all but inevitable if the denomination did not vote to change course at the next General Convention. They also warned that even the 2008 Lambeth Conference of Anglican bishops in Canterbury might be affected.

Archbishop Drexel W. Gomez of the Diocese of the West Indies said the American denomination is teaching a "new gospel" that is unclear about God's nature and affirms cultural values, even when they run counter to historic Christianity.

"The primates will decide" if they consider the response of the Episcopal Church "adequate," he said. Gomez added, however, that he expected no change in the stance of the Episcopal Church when it comes to gays.

"It will be up to us to try to sort out the mess," he said. "Given our present mood, the convention will most certainly be followed by some action. We have worked too hard, too long, to leave it like that.

"Anglicanism is really now in a state of flux. ... We are being forced into this by people who are teaching something new and something totally different," he said.

Chung said that, "If the Episcopal Church does not repent and follow what the primates have asked ... I think many of the [conservative archbishops] will have to assess their own position whether Lambeth 2008 is a place we want to be."

Afterword

The "Hope and a Future" conference spurred continued growth in the confessing and renewal groups in this country, and other dramatic developments also occurred.

By the end of January 2006, for example, the Anglican Communion Network reported that it had grown to include more than 1,000 parishes, 2,500 clergy, 10 dioceses and six convocations, representing an estimated 250,000 members.

On the heels of the conference, four Episcopal Church (USA) congregations in northeast Ohio voted to sever their ties with the denomination and affiliate with the Diocese of Bolivia in South America, the *Akron Beacon-Journal* reported.

The paper stated that the four congregations were leaving because of "divergent understandings of the authority of Scripture and traditional Christian teaching."

Their decisions followed similar votes by six Episcopal congregations in the Episcopal Diocese of Florida, which is based in Jacksonville. The Florida congregations voted to align with the newly formed Anglican Alliance of North Florida.

Representatives of the congregations in Ohio and Florida – and representatives in other denominations – are discussing property and other issues with denominational officials. In previous cases, those officials and the denominations have attempted to prevent departing congregations from keeping their property.

In California, a Superior Court judge ruled that the Episcopal Church (USA) had no right to take over the property of three congregations, which voted to leave the denomination and join conservative Anglican bodies.

By February 2006, it was reported that 34 congregations in 16 states had voted to leave the Episcopal Church (USA).

Meanwhile, a renewal group reported in March 2006 that 97 congregations in 19 states had left the United Church of Christ since the denomination voted to sanction same-gender marriages during its national governing body meeting in July 2005.

Speaking to a group in Andover Congregational Church in New Hampshire, the Rev. Dr. Bob Thompson of Corinth Reformed Church in Hickory, N.C., said the UCC has a "crisis of lost churches, lost funds and lost unity brought about by the actions of our national leadership," *The Manchester Union Leader* reported.

Thompson is the leader of Faithful and Welcoming Churches of the United Church of Christ, an evangelical renewal organization that is tracking the exodus of churches. "We publish the list not to encourage other churches to follow suit; but rather to note the seriousness of the current crisis in the UCC."

Other developments were occurring in the Presbyterian Church (USA), where the pastors of four congregations in western Pennsylvania formed what they call the first ministry network in their denomination for mutual support, encouragement and joint ministry.

There also was the spectacular growth of the Confessing Church Movement within the denomination, which, in its first year, grew to 11.1 percent of the denomination's 11,178 congregations and 16.33 percent of its 2.56 million members.

And groups such as the New Wineskins Initiative, the Presbyterian Global Fellowship, the cooperation of 16 ministries through the Presbyterian Renewal Network and others are growing as they work for a return to classical Christian teaching of the Biblical faith.

Across the Protestant mainline denominations, the work of many groups – such as the Confessing Movement in the United Methodist Church, the WordAlone Network in the Evangelical Lutheran Church in America and others – is indicative of this movement to associate with like-minded believers in traditional, orthodox Christianity.

One of the most telling examples is the Association for Church Renewal, an association of executives and leaders of more than 30 church renewal organizations and ministries that are related to the mainline denominations in the United States and Canada. Its founding purpose statement says that the group is "an association to encourage and support renewal and reform leaders from the 'mainline' denominations, assisting them in developing their ministries' witness to orthodox Christianity in both church and society."

More conferences, networks, joint worship services, missions and youth activities built around the questions "Who do you say that I am?" and "Choose you this day" are planned across the Protestant mainline denominations in the future. That may be the coming Reformation in America or, as Episcopal Bishop Robert W. Duncan Jr. said:

"We are continuing to deal with choosing Jesus first: Jesus above culture, Jesus above comfort, Jesus above property, Jesus above family and friends, Jesus above any other security, Jesus above a wayward North American Church. We are here to confirm our choice for truth above accommodation."

Printed in the United States
52341LVS00002B/154-306

9 780971 191952